Purge & Bloom

By Brooks Decker

ISBN:979-8-9891531-3-8

Published by Quillkeepers Press, LLC
PO Box 10236
Casa Grande, AZ 85130

For mom, dad, and Travis, who are irrevocably woven into every side of my story.

Purge

Bloom

Purge

1999

Remember when phones were attached to houses?
Literal lines to hold us, tie us up in whatever nuclear
family disaster we wish we hadn't come from just to
speak to the cute boy from second period.

Remember the internet just birthed?
Dial-up noises screaming like a new baby,
world beginning to touch our fingertips, pervs
wild with glee, anonymity, opportunity to make
fantasy reality with no consequence.

The toilet bowl of Y2K.
Nineties grunge ushering us young, drunk,
jaded into a new millennium or apocalypse,
won't know till midnight. We were scared of
everything and nothing, aching for open road,
arms to hold us, an entire lifetime worth of
mistakes just waiting to be made.

Remember when phones were attached to houses?
I miss their ring, the way they tethered me to something real.

Since Birth

I have heavy laid under the burden of a man's
indiscretions, the weight of his secrets spilled onto
me, into me, making brittle bones, solemn spirit.

Little girl hair twirled, stroked, by adult hands who
held no regard for its softness, or acknowledged
eyes squeezed shut against the ritual itself.
If I believe I am asleep I am only dreaming.

Then and also, crushed by invisibility. The
weight of absence perhaps heaviest of all.
Chasing daddy, love in motion. I only ever
have him by the skin of my teeth, flailing.

So, I paint boys into men, beg them love me,
never quite enough to curb their hunger for
more than a moment. A dog crying for scraps
commands more dignity.

Then and also, a wife. A drunken stupor.
A dirty magazine. An infidelity. A decade of
good years worn thin from the friction of my
hope against his selfishness; quiet breaking of
my spirit piece by piece, every time we writhe in
the same familiar pit of which has stained us year
after year. A promise to God to bear the burden
of a man's indiscretions, till death do us part.

Hypochondria

Death is always in front of me.
On long car rides, short ones,
over bridges, underpasses, in
margaritas, cigarettes, Tylenol,
antibiotics, fast food, processed
cereal, and turning left when
I meant to go right.
Men working construction.
Men walking down streets.
Men in parking lots.
Handle of the grocery cart,
planes to places foreign, domestic,
movie theatres, schools, malls.
My bed, my shower, my kitchen,
every headache, every twitch.
Death is always in front of me.
I wish he had somewhere else to be.

Certain

Back and forth between
freedom and Egypt,
asking for directions
despite the map being
branded on my palms.
Have you ever stood
on the edge of a cliff
certain you would never
jump, but sick to your
stomach because in your
heart you've leapt
a thousand times?

Nothing New

Once upon a time
I kept a sailor's mouth
and sirens song,
quick to flip scripts,
and if loose lips sink
ships, my hips spoke
enough for all of me.
I bore honey, honey.
Once upon a time
I was a skeleton key,
nothing unique in the
pattern of me, played out
song, birthright gone wrong.
All that honey spilled for flies.

As If

Chasing relevancy as if it can be caught.
As if it is low tide, and given enough
time, the universe will thrust it forward,
wash it over your feet for you to revel in,
basking in its glory. As if it has glory.
As if it makes something of you.

Open House

Flung wide
screen door pulls,
anointed oil
covers walls,
demons swept
onto grass,
I am a loosed woman.
Soil colored secrets,
poured out
drunkards spew.
Past made puddles,
I am empty of
who I was.
Ash covered
torn sackcloth,
fist beating concrete.
You must not
leave me vacant.
I will not be
an open house.

Your Name Here

There was a boy I
did not notice once
until he noticed me.
I blinked at his hello,
then cotton candy,
corn dogs, an open door.
He was a treasure map,
confetti at a wedding,
what's new pussycat.

I spilled all over his floor.

We danced all night in
rooms foggy with
cigarette smoke, drove
slow, windows down.
He was light made dark
by my own unceasing
tug at his shirt hems.

I begged him sop me up.

Used to like to think
he couldn't.
Understand now
he didn't want to.

Eager

She throws herself on his altar,
a sacrifice appalled by fire, the
scent of her own burning and
his walking away the moment
she becomes consumed. She
begs him wait, mad woman,
hollering about pressure turning
coal to diamonds. He is cheap,
impatient, caring nothing about
diamonds or any other precious
thing. She forfeits all her fruit at
first shake of the tree. Now he is
full, she is empty.

Panic Attack

Mid-sentence on earth, then,
What if my brain forgets to
tell my lungs to breathe?
Blast off.
It is suddenly very hot.
Did you know people can
spontaneously combust?
I read an article about it.
There was an illustration, a
lady in a chair charred black
exploded, legs still intact.
Orthopedic leather shoes.
I'm still talking, it's automatic.
Legs up, legs down, sweater
off, then on. These people
probably think I am on drugs.
I wish I was.
I talk from space for two hours.
My car is re-entry, but
I still keep reminding my brain
to tell my lungs to breathe.

Their Patience

You hold me in Your crook,
crease wet with my mess.
You tell me, *be still.*
I want to desperately, but
am all knocking limbs,
gnashing teeth, a thick paste
of gonna and didn't.
You tell me *listen,*
but I have too much to say,
an irrational fear of losing my
voice, throat gone anaphylaxis.
You attempt to shuffle me
towards the promise of my
potential. I kick, scream,
throw myself to the ground.
Toddler with hips and breasts,
knows best.

Resignation

It isn't anger.
I left anger in
every bedroom
we've fallen asleep in,
theme parks,
childhood homes,
cars both moving and parked,
distant lands,
soaking other people's linens,
phone lines, text messages, email,
professional buildings
where someone sat
between us nodding,
sipping warm liquid.
It isn't anger.
It is worse.

The Sailor's Wife II (2020)

Contentment, meet despair. Waltz, resigned but still hungry,
feeding on crumbs from a stranger's table, careful not to bite
the hand that feeds. I swallow back the rage of uncertainty
over and over and all at once, with a slow blink, closed lip grin.

Blessed are those who trust in the Lord.

Fattened calf, meet belly of the whale. Slow drag, hot house
writhing, ache of loneliness rubbed raw against terror of
incompetence. I sweat out demons and name them, from
beds,
hospital rooms, elementary school cafeterias, the front seat
of my car in a mall parking lot.

Resist the devil and he will flee from you.

Love, meet war. First dance made mosh pit, romance left to
choke on reality, distance mauling trust, time zone drunk with
nothing to talk about. I scream into pillows and call my
mother.
Drive to Atlanta to sit at my father's table. I share my bed with
my children. Close my eyes every night. Open them every
morning.

Come to me all who are weary and burdened,
and I will give you rest.

Bloom

Whatever Is Convenient

I love god dressed as self.
My own intuitive knowing, and
internal divinity, the ultimate truth.
Until my divinity appears to have a
personality disorder, and truth is, I am
botched chaos, a flailing incompetent
dumpster fire with daddy issues.
Then I prefer God of the universe.
They who
manage the tide,
cracking open of seeds,
aerodynamics of bumble bees,
slowing of my anxious heart,
softening of my cynicism,
forgiveness of my shitty divinity.

Soma

The body keeps
score, but you
have permission to
become,
become,
become.
Wildflower bloom
in Gehenna,
seeds scavenging
for fertile ground.
Blossom cares not
about dross.

Mind Over Matter

I wish I had
learned sooner,
the space
between my ears,
is so much
more sensitive,
than the space
between my legs.

Sunday Morning Haiku

Expectations on
pause, I, hesitant, unfurl.
Light cracks through blinds, closed.

Becoming, a Bop

She is on the cusp of forty,
aching for expansion, tired of
folding herself tiny, origami.
She longs to take up space.
Becoming small is not noble.
Self-doubt is not humility.

Trees do not belong in pots.

She is ripe but watches
failure watch her from the
back of every room. A ghost,
a person, a premonition, a
chorus of *you do not belong
here* and *you're too much,
never enough.* Sticky tunes stay,
replay. World's worst mixtape.

Trees do not belong in pots.

She edges towards discomfort, one
foot in front of other, doddling. A
cacophony of color, words, she
teeters between linger and leap.
Filling herself out, she dilates.
Uncertainty can be a springboard.

Trees do not belong in pots.

Air Plants

Tillandsia like tiny tumbleweed
sweep across hectic highway.
Forward, backward, forward.
Florida flora turned toddler,
learning to cross the street.

They require almost nothing.
No soil, root, host. Just space
to sit, grow. A sip of dew now,
later, soon, never. Comfortable
tucked against a tree, rolling
along highway, ornamentally
potted on a side table in your
grandma's palatial sunroom.

Wherever they land, they flourish.

Hush

I long to be quiet.
You cannot hear
flowering,
or the breath of
evaporating dew
from dawn's
ground.
Sun does not
screech,
moon does not
sigh.
It is possible
to be both
silent and heard.

Conversation With Self

I want to talk about jasmine, how it's all I smell,
whole planet a wild climbing plant in bloom.
I want to talk about fall, how it was always my favorite,
about the time I planned to compose an entire volume of
poetry about a boy who couldn't love me, called
Two Years of October and Things Inevitably One Sided.

I want to talk about how I like spring best now,
no longer feel fastened to dying a million deaths.
How I am more rapt by jasmine, azaleas, sleepy
annuals stretching awake, breaking winter's ground,
opening their eyes, leaning towards sun. I want to talk about
the startling goodness of rebirth, born anew every morning.

Form, a Triolet

Body is a map,
both fettered and free,
never a mishap,
body is a map,
comparison trap,
allow her to be.
Body is a map,
both fettered and free.

A Moment in Middleburg

Wires buzz above. Electricity conducts,
energy born, sent tightrope walking.
Human hand harnessed power made
static noise. Ground dewy wet with
morning's cool breath, oxeye daisies
sprout fragile tendrils, gently caressing
tossed garbage, bottles and cans
nurtured by consistent growth of
earth uninhibited. Flesh and blood
absentmindedly annihilating God's opus.
Opus singing back in seed and sigh,
a fortitude unimaginable.

Midsummer

Nothing more inspiring than a
woman sure, present in her skin.
Kinky curls jut out in every
direction, bangs matted down by
humidity. Breasts loose, slung
low, nipples free to point, retreat.
Colorful cotton pulls against belly
round, button like third eye,
sneaks a peek. Prickly legs, last
shaven some Sunday ago, thighs
press against themselves, protectors
of ripe treasures, folds bearing gold.
She smiles wide, laughs loud, floats
across floors unbridled. Sultry, divine
goddess, sure of nothing except herself.

Satisfied

He casts a wide net
around me. Pulls in
what bobs along surface,
what has buried itself below.

He grips all four of my corners,
sprawls himself beneath my feet.
Flesh of man made solid ground,
reminds me I am sturdy, strong.

He loosens me,
shakes me out.
Wound woman uncoiled,
spring become slinky.
His ease takes my hand,
smiles, invites me in.

He is home.
Imperfect Eden.
Closest I'll ever be to
agape,
this side of eternity.

Blessed Fall

I am Felix Culpa.
One grave mistake
after another,
footfall measured
blunder by blunder.
Catastrophes drenched
in grace, reborn
happy endings.

Purge & Bloom

Brooks Decker is a writer, artist, and mental health professional in Jacksonville Florida. She may be found walking the St. Johns River, treasure hunting at various thrift stores, swinging through Starbucks with one or both of her teenagers, front porch sitting with her husband, and ceaselessly assessing her relentless faith despite the perpetual pecking of existential dread. This is her first book.